Copyright © 2020 Educate Through Nate
'COOKING WITH DADDIES'
ISBN: 978-988-74044-6-0 (paperback)
ISBN: 978-988-74045-3-8 (eBook)

All Rights Reserved. No part of this book may be reproduced or used in any manner without written permission of the copright owner except for the use of quotations in a book review.

Published in Hong Kong by Melissa Jane Lavi

Copyrighted Material

Finding happiness
in
EVERY THING
EVERY WHERE
EVERY DAY!

Hello again, my name is Nate,
and a very good day to you.
We're about to make some pasta.
Come along and join us too.

Daddy '2' likes spicy.
Daddy '1' does not like spice.

I love pasta any way.
As long as it tastes nice.

Daddy '1' chops onions,
in pieces small and square.
The onions always make him cry.
But he says he doesn't care.

Daddy '2' adds garlic,
and some thick tomato paste.
The smell begins to fill the air,
as it passes by my face.

I'm still too young to cook myself,
so I sit there by their sides.
Watching as they chop and stir,
with big, wide, open eyes.

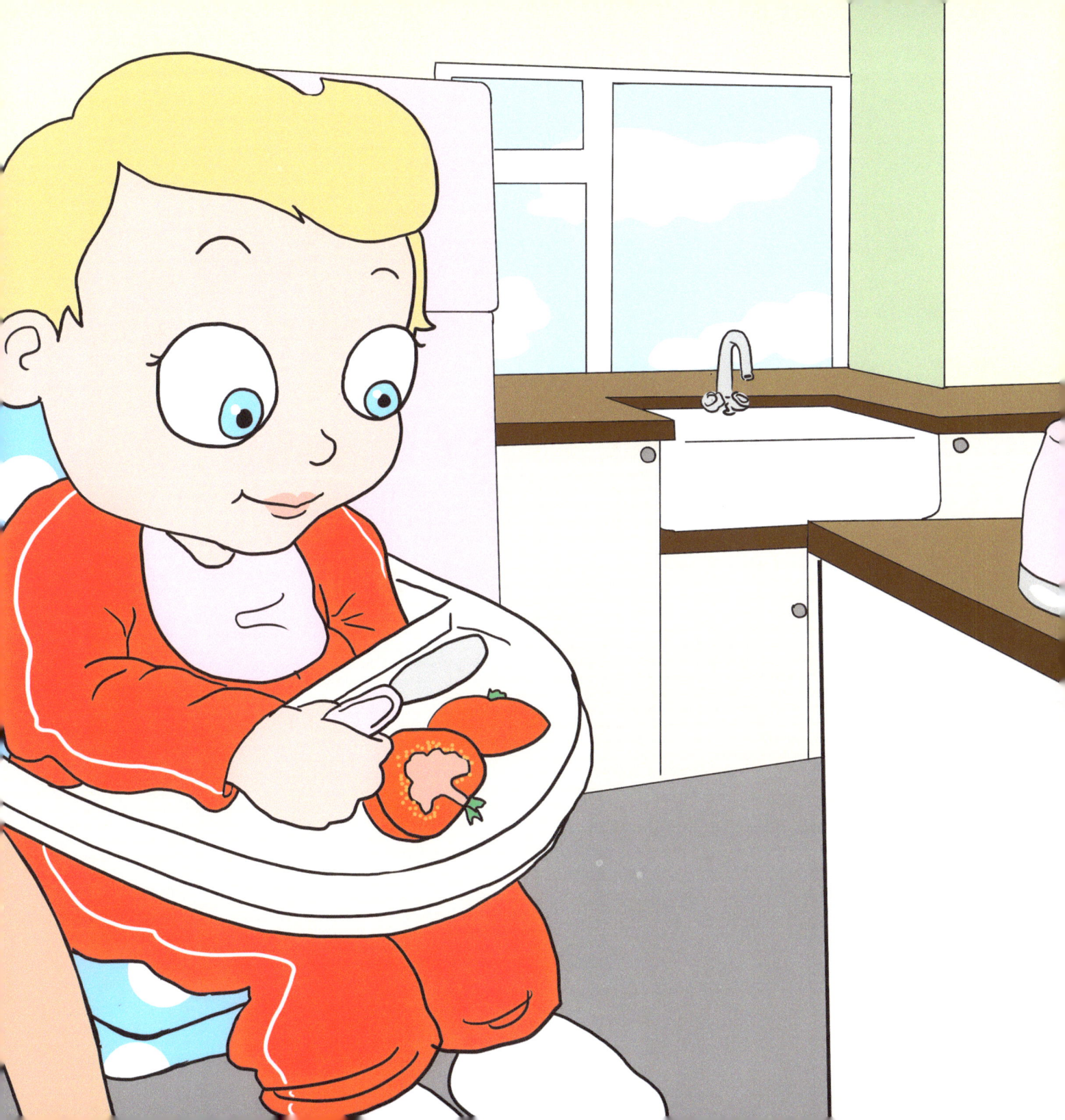

And now the war of spices,
as they simply can't agree.
Daddy '2' adds chilli,
while Daddy '1' can't see.

We've reached the final stages.
The sauce will soon be done.
They add a touch of 'this' and 'that',
and call us all to come.

I have a friend for dinner, and her parents '1' and '2'.

And Uncle Jay is also here.
He loves our pasta too.

The sauce looks so delicious.
A bright and vibrant red.

We can not wait to lap it up,
with a squishy slice of bread.

The salad, green and crunchy,
so inviting to the eye.
With a slightly tangy dressing,
that we can not wait to try.

There's only one thing missing,
on this lovely, yummy plate.
They forgot to make the pasta,
AND NOW WE HAVE TO WAIT!

SILLY OLD DADDIES!

My name is Nate, and life is great,
with Daddy '1' and '2'.

Be sure to come and play again,
as we still have lots to do.

But now, for me, it's bath time,
as there's pasta in my hair.

Tomorrow is a brand new day.
I can't wait to see you there.

www.ingramcontent.com/pod-product-compliance
Lightning Source LLC
LaVergne TN
LVHW070441070526
838199LV00036B/677